I. INTRODUCTION

In a recent study of horizontal collusion and conspiracy cases brought by the Federal Trade Commission (FTC) in the 1980's, we found that only 50 percent of the cases could be explained by traditional collusion theories of setting price or restraining output (Langenfeld and Morris, 1990a). Another 17 percent of the cases could be explained by recent theories of raising rivals' costs; that is, by one group of competitors taking actions to competitively disadvantage another group of competitors. That leaves 33 percent of the cases unexplained by the standard anticompetitive theories presented in the literature. We also found that about one quarter of the cases involved agreements on advertising restrictions, such as agreements not to advertise prices. The industries involved ranged from physicians to automobile dealers and totalled more than $400 billion of commerce in 1982.

There is an extensive literature on advertising, much of which is applicable to predicting the effects of advertising restrictions. To show that an advertising restriction is an anticompetitive practice, it is necessary to show that the restriction raises the profits of the members adhering to the restriction and how consumers are harmed by the restriction. Benham (1972) and Bond et al. (1980) argue that restrictions disadvantage certain competitors. The reduced competition from the disadvantaged competitors leads to higher profits for incumbent firms and higher prices to consumers. Friedman (1983) presents a model where raising the costs of sending advertising messages can lead to higher profits by reducing total advertising expenditures. If advertising is totally predatory (i.e., affects only market shares, not total sales), the restriction will raise profits. Another set of work posits that advertising restrictions raise search costs. In one form, advertising restrictions raises the costs of consumers searching for products and sellers (Maurizi and Kelly, 1978). With higher search costs, consumers search less and become less sensitive to differences in relative prices; that is, the demand for each individual firm becomes less elastic. With the less elastic demand, firms naturally raise their prices and reduce output.[1] In another form, advertising restrictions essentially raise the costs of firms looking for customers, resulting in less elastic demands and higher prices. (Butters, 1977; Grossman and Shapiro, 1984; Tirole, 1988, pp. 292-294).

This paper shows how competitors can use advertising restrictions as "rent increasing costs" to raise prices and harm consumers. Rent increasing costs are those costs which raise rents as they increase. Nelson (1957) was the first to recognize these costs when he showed that under certain conditions the returns to a fixed factor of production would increase with increases in the price of a variable input. Using Nelson's fundamental insight, Salop, Scheffman and Schwartz (1984) recognized the possibility that firms could use the regulatory process to raise their costs and increase profits. Independent of Nelson (1957),

---

[1] There is a wide literature on equilibrium price dispersion in markets with search costs (e.g, Diamond (1971), Butters (1977), Varian (1980), Stahl (1989)). Of these, only Butters (1977) directly considers the effect of advertising. In his model, increases in the cost of sending advertising messages to consumers leads to fewer messages and fewer informed consumers. Fewer informed consumers leads to a shift in the equilibrium price distribution so that the minimum, average, and maximum prices increase.

Maloney, McCormick, and Tollison (1979) hypothesized that firms could benefit from organized labor because unions effectively restricted output and raised prices. Langenfeld and Morris (1990b) and Scheffman (1991) explained how rent increasing costs are important in the context of antitrust.

This paper extends the previous literature in two respects. Section II provides a more general formulation for when cost increases are profitable. We find that fixed factors of production are not a necessary condition for profitable cost increases. All that is necessary is that marginal costs rise to a sufficient amount above the increase in average costs to compensate firms for fewer sales. Section III then shows that advertising restrictions can behave as rent increasing costs. First we review some search cost models and show that they fit within the theory of rent increasing costs. We then demonstrate that advertising in the framework of Stigler and Becker (1977) and Spence (1980) can act as a rent increasing cost. Following the procedure used by Spence, the framework is changed to one similar to homogeneous goods. The analysis of rent increasing costs can then be applied directly to the modified framework. In contrast to search cost explanations, the analysis shows that advertising restrictions can lead to increases in sales as measured by the quantity of goods sold. Although the units sold may increase, value to consumers decreases because they receive less information about the goods that they purchase.

II. RENT INCREASING COSTS

In this section we develop the theory of rent increasing costs. The analysis starts with the initial equilibrium of price-taking competitors. By price-taking competitors we mean that each firm assumes that if it restricts output at the market price, another firm will make the sale instead. The inverse market demand is represented by $P(X)$ where the market output (X) is the sum of the individual firm outputs, x_i. We also make the simplifying assumption that the firms are all identical. The production cost of each firm is represented by $C(x_i, \phi)$ and marginal cost is represented by C_x. C is continuous, twice differentiable in both x and ϕ, and convex in x. The parameter ϕ represents a cost parameter and we assume that $C_\phi > 0$.

The profits of each firm are given by:

$$\pi(x_i) - P(X) - C(x_i).$$

Because there are N identical firms acting as price takers, the output of each firm is determined by where the market price equals marginal cost. That is,

$$P(N \cdot x_i^*) \equiv C_x(x_i^*, \phi), \tag{1}$$

where $x_i^* \equiv x_i^*(\phi, N)$, and N is the number of firms. To simplify the notation, we initially suppress N and let $x_i^* = x_i^*(\phi)$. The total profit of the firms in the market is given by:

4

$$\Pi(\phi) \equiv N \cdot [P(Nx_i) \cdot x_i - C(x_i, \phi)]$$
$$\equiv N \cdot [P(Nx_i^{\cdot}) \cdot x_i^{\cdot} - C(x_i^{\cdot}, \phi)] \qquad (2)$$
$$\equiv N \cdot [C_x(x_i^{\cdot}, \phi) \cdot x_i^{\cdot} - C(x_i^{\cdot}, \phi)].$$

We wish to determine the necessary conditions for the cost increase to be profitable. A cost increase is profitable as long as $\partial \Pi / \partial \phi > 0$. Differentiating (2) with respect to ϕ and rearranging, we have a cost increase is profitable as long as:

$$C_{x\phi} + C_{xx}x_{i\phi}^{\cdot} > \frac{C_\phi}{x_i^{\cdot}}. \qquad (3)$$

The right hand side of (3) is the increase in average costs from increasing ϕ, holding x_i constant. The first term on the left hand side is the vertical change in marginal costs from increasing ϕ and the second term is the movement along the marginal cost curve. Therefore, the left hand side gives the change in price given a change in ϕ. This can be verified by differentiating (1) with respect to ϕ giving:

$$C_{x\phi} + C_{xx}x_{i\phi}^{\cdot} \equiv P_x Nx_{i\phi}^{\cdot}. \qquad (4)$$

In words, (3) implies that the cost increase will be profitable when raising ϕ increases price faster than the increase in average costs.

For the cost increase to be profitable, the cost increase must raise marginal costs which in turn raises price.[2] Moreover, we can specify the amount of the increase. Solving (4) for $x_{i\phi}^{\bullet}$, substituting into (3), and rearranging gives:

$$C_{x\phi} > \frac{C_{\phi}}{x_i^{\bullet}} \left[1 - \frac{\epsilon^d}{\epsilon^s} \right] \tag{5}$$

where ϵ^d is the demand elasticity and ϵ^s is the supply elasticity. The demand elasticity is negative therefore and the right hand side term in parentheses is greater than 1. Accordingly, for (5) to hold, it is necessary that the increase in marginal costs be greater than the increase in average costs. It also follows from (5) that for cost increases which raise marginal costs relative to average costs, the cost increase is more likely to be profitable the less elastic the demand and the more elastic the supply.[3] Accordingly, we have the following proposition:

PROPOSITION 1: *For price taking firms, cost increases that raise marginal costs to a greater extent than average costs may raise profits. A profit increase is more likely the less elastic the market demand and the more elastic the market supply.*

Notice that our result is more general than Nelson's which applied only to the price of a variable input in the presence of fixed factors. Fixed factors are

---

[2] The assumptions on the cost function do not rule out that marginal costs decline with increases in ϕ ($C_{x\phi} < 0$). For example, an environmental regulation may mandate new technology with higher fixed costs but lower marginal costs. But because price is equal to marginal cost, and marginal costs must increase for a profitable cost increase.

[3] As a special case, notice that when the firms have no market power ($\epsilon^d = \infty$), no cost increase would be profitable.

6

not necessary for our result. For instance, consider the following production function with decreasing returns to scale:

$$x_i = L_i^{\frac{1}{4}} K_i^{\frac{1}{4}},$$

where L_i represents firm i's use of labor and K_i represents firm i's use of capital. Let w represent the price of labor and r represent the price of capital. Then, the cost function is given by:

$$c(x_i, w, r) = 2 w^{\frac{1}{2}} r^{\frac{1}{2}} x_i^2.$$

Finally, let demand be represented by $P = a - bX$.

Using (5), we have that raising either the price of labor or capital is profitable as long as:

$$b > \frac{4 w^{\frac{1}{2}} r^{\frac{1}{2}}}{N}, \tag{6}$$

where N is the number of firms in the market. The left hand side of (6) is the absolute value of the slope of the demand curve. The right hand side of (6) is the slope of the market supply curve. Thus, for the cost function and linear demand, it would be profitable to raise an input price as long as the market demand curve is steeper than the slope of the market supply curve. It is not necessary for capital to be fixed for a market-wide wage increase to be profitable.

7

Although we have assumed a constant number of firms, this assumption is not necessary for a cost increase to be profitable. Suppose the cost functions were of the form $C(x_i, \phi) = F_i + c(x_i, \phi)$ and F_i is distributed over $(0, \infty)$. Then there will be a supply schedule of firms willing to enter the market. Letting the subscript i index firms from the lowest F to the highest, the number of firms in the market would be given by:

$$F_N \leq \frac{C(x_i^*(\phi, N), \phi)}{x_i^*(\phi, N)} < F_{N+1}.$$

A cost increase may still be profitable to the N incumbent firms. If ϵ^d in expression (5) is taken to be the residual demand curve facing the incumbent firms (i.e., consumer demand less the amount supplied by entrants), then it still gives the condition under which a cost increase would be profitable for the incumbents.

III. ADVERTISING RESTRICTIONS

In this section we enrich the extant literature by showing how advertising expenditures behave as rent increasing costs. If advertising expenditures are rent increasing costs, then it would be profitable for an association of competitors to restrict or raise the costs of advertising. By raising the cost of advertising, we mean that the marginal cost of supplying information to a consumer increases. Accordingly, a restriction on the lowest cost advertising media would raise the cost of advertising. A restriction on advertising content which makes it more difficult to communicate information to consumers also would raise the cost of advertising. Further, our use of "advertising" is not limited to communication through broadcast or print media. When a dentist conducts a seminar on dental hygiene for youth at the local YMCA, she is advertising the location, usefulness, and type of service that she offers.

Grossman and Shapiro (1984) and Tirole (1988, pp. 292-94) have shown that increases in the cost of advertising price and location can raise profits; therefore, advertising can function as a rent increasing cost within their framework. Tirole's model is interesting because higher costs of informing consumers leads to increases in total advertising expenditures. This result is in contrast with the common perception that advertising restrictions are profitable because they result in lower advertising expenditures. Although cost reduction may motivate a restriction when advertising is mainly predatory, it is not likely to be the only motive. The "cost reduction" explanation tends to predict unchanged or lower prices with advertising restrictions (Friedman, 1983; Schneider, Klein, and Murphy, 1981), but many studies have shown that advertising restrictions often raise prices.[4] Search costs models, as well as the model presented below, all predict higher prices from higher advertising costs, suggesting that cost reduction is not the sole motive for advertising restrictions.

---

[4] See, for example, Benham (1972); Bond et al. (1980); Cady (1976); Kwoka (1984); Maurizi and Kelly (1978); Schroeter et al. (1987).

Before going on to our model of advertising restrictions, we wish to suggest a reason why advertising restrictions are likely to serve as rent increasing costs. Consider the advertising technology described in Butters (1977). As seller sends S advertising messages. The messages randomly reach a target population of M consumers and each consumer has an equal likelihood of receiving an advertisement. For many messages and consumers, the likelihood that a consumer receives no messages is approximated by:

$$1 - \Phi - e^{-\frac{S}{M}}$$

and Φ gives the faction of consumers that receive at least one advertisement. The cost of reaching $M\Phi$ consumers therefore is:

$$C(M,\Phi,p_s) - p_s M \ln\left(\frac{1}{1-\Phi}\right)$$

where p_s is the price of sending an advertising message. Raising the price of a message leads to a greater increase in marginal costs of informing consumers than the increase in average costs. This is easily shown by:

$$C_{\Phi p_s} - \frac{M}{(1-\Phi)^3} > \frac{M\ln\left(\frac{1}{1-\Phi}\right)}{\Phi} - \frac{C_{p_s}}{\Phi}$$

Therefore, given proper demand and production cost conditions, advertising expenditures may be rent increasing costs within the search cost framework. Below we show that advertising restrictions can behave as rent increasing costs

10

when advertising provides information that increases the value of using heterogenous goods.

A.   The model

In the framework of Stigler and Becker (1977) and Spence (1980), advertising enters consumers' utility functions. Advertising provides information that makes consumption easier, more enjoyable, more efficient, or more effective. For some examples, advertising may: inform consumers of the proper way to use a product (e.g., Q-Tip advertisements); provide consumption attributes (e.g., cigarette advertisements); or lead to more effect use of consumers' time (e.g., advertisements to see a dermatologist for a prescription for Rogaine). Following Spence's procedure, we convert the model of heterogeneous goods to one similar to homogeneous goods. From the modified framework, we then demonstrate how advertising restrictions can be a profitable cost-raising strategy for associations of competitors.

Let the aggregate consumer value function for a group of n competing goods be

$$V(m) = \int_0^m B(s)\, ds \qquad (7)$$

where

$$m - \sum_{j=1}^{n} \frac{A(a_j;\theta) x_j^{\alpha}}{\alpha}, \qquad\qquad (8)$$

and where $B(\cdot)$ is a decreasing scaler function, x_j are the physical sales in units

of product j by firm j, $j = 1, \ldots, n$, a_j are the advertising expenditures of firm

j, $A(\cdot;\theta)$ is a function that relates advertising expenditures to consumer benefits

$(A_a > 0)$, θ is a parameter reflecting the efficacy of advertising expenditures

$(A_\theta > 0)$, and α is another demand parameter.[5] In the absence of income effects,

the inverse demands are given by:

$$p_i - \frac{\partial V}{\partial x_i} - B(m)A(a_i)x_i^{\alpha-1}$$

The revenues of firm i are $p_i x_i$. Therefore, the profit function of firm i is:

$$\pi_i - B(m)A(a_i)x_i^{\alpha} - C(x_i) - a_i$$

where $C(\cdot)$ is the production cost of x_i.[6]

To turn the analysis into one similar to homogeneous products, let $y_i = A(a_i)x_i^{\alpha}$, $i = 1, \ldots, n$. With this new set of variables,

---

[5] To convert the model to the Stigler and Becker model, let $\alpha = 1$. See Stigler and Becker (1977), p. 84, equation (13).

[6] Given the assumptions on demand and costs, the model is also applicable to the situation of choosing product quality when the quality attribute is a public good in production. For example, improving the clarity of an IO textbook by additional editing would be an improvement in quality. As long as the editing does not significantly change the length of the textbook, the editing is a fixed cost and does not affect marginal production costs.

$$\pi_i = B(m)y_i - g(y_i, a_i),$$

where

$$m = \frac{1}{\alpha} \sum_{j=1}^{n} y_j,$$

and the costs are

$$g(y_i, a_i) = C\left[\left[\frac{y_i}{A(a_i)} \right]^{\frac{1}{\alpha}} \right] + a_i. \tag{9}$$

With this transformation, this problem is similar to a single homogeneous good, where y_i is the output of firm i and the industry inverse demand is $B(m)$. One interpretation of this transformation is that y is a commodity in consumers' utility functions and x_i, $i = 1, \ldots, n$, are market goods used to produce y and the information $A(a_i)$, $i = 1, \ldots, n$, also enters the consumer production function (Stigler and Becker, 1977). $B(m)$ then gives the consumers' inverse demand for y.

For each level of output y_i, firm i will select advertising expenditures to minimize total costs.[7] Let $a_i(y_i)$ represent the cost minimizing advertising expenditures for a given level of y_i. Then the cost function can be restated as $h(y_i; \theta) = g(y_i, a_i(y_i))$.

---

[7] Within this modified model, selecting advertising expenditures (a_i) is analogous to selecting the cost minimizing production scale when additional fixed expenditures lowers marginal costs.

The effect of an advertising restriction depends upon the rivalrous interaction of firms in the market. In terms of our analysis, a "price-taking" assumption would mean that each firm assumes that $B(m)$ is constant. This price-taking assumption, however, may not adequately reflect the markets that we are considering which have heterogeneous goods. This can be accounted for by utilizing a Nash conjecture in our analysis. That is, each firm only considers its direct effect on $B(m)$ and ignores the potential actions of rivals.

The parameter θ reflects the efficacy of advertising expenditures. That is, as θ increases each dollar spent on advertising provides a greater amount of valuable information to consumers. Thus, in the Butters advertising technology stated above, θ would be inversely related to the price of sending a message (i.e., $\theta = -p_s$). An advertising restriction limits firms' abilities to supply information to consumers so that each dollar spent on advertising provides consumers with less information. Hence, to study the ability of advertising restrictions to raise profits, we will see whether an association of competitors has the incentive to restrict θ assuming that the association could do so at no additional cost.

B.   *B(m)* constant

In our analysis, $B(m)$ plays the role of an inverse demand curve. Holding the output of all other firms constant, then $B(m)$ falls as firm i increases output y_i. In general, however, firms will react to actions by firm i. If the sum for the reactions are so great that firm i believes or acts as if $B(m)$ is constant, then the

14

model is analogous to the model of price-taking behavior with homogeneous goods in Section II.

We now make the simplifying assumption that firms have the same cost function $h(y_i, \theta)$. Because there are n similar firms acting as price takers, the output of each firm is determined by:

$$B(\frac{1}{\alpha} \cdot \sum_{j=1}^{n} y_j^*) \equiv h_y(y_i^*, \theta) .$$ (10)

where $y_i^* \equiv y_i^*(\theta)$. Also for simplicity, we assume that an association can enforce an advertising restriction at no cost. The association will try to maximize the total profits of its members:

$$\Pi(\theta) \equiv n \cdot [B(m) \cdot y_i - h(y_i, \theta)]$$

$$\equiv n \cdot [B(\frac{1}{\alpha} \cdot \sum_{j=1}^{n} y_j^{\bullet}) \cdot y_i^{\bullet} - h(y_i^{\bullet}, \theta)] \tag{11}$$

$$\equiv n \cdot [h_y(y_i^{\bullet}, \theta) \cdot y_i^{\bullet} - h(y_i^{\bullet}, \theta)].$$

Therefore, we have constructed a situation where firms act as perfect competitors with respect to their value-output decisions, yet the firms are able to collude and act as a monopolist with respect the form or effectiveness of advertising.[8]

The association has the incentive to restrict advertising (decrease θ) if the total profits of the association are decreasing as θ increases ($\partial \Pi / \partial \theta < 0$). By differentiating Π with respect to θ and rearranging, we find that an association has an incentive to restrict advertising (decrease θ) as long as

$$h_{y\theta} + h_{yy} y_{i\theta}^{\bullet} < \frac{h_{\theta}}{y_i^{\bullet}}. \tag{12}$$

In words, the restraint is profitable as long as the fall in average costs of supplying y value to consumers from increasing θ is less than the decline in

---

[8] For several reasons firms may find cost-based strategies such as advertising restrictions preferable to directly restricting output and raising price. Any agreement to raise price must be policed by the group. Secret price cuts or sales may defeat such an agreement, especially when a large number of competitors are involved. Advertising restrictions may reduce this problem because it is probably easier to detect a firm advertising than it is to detect a selective price cut. In addition, agreements that directly limit output directly or fix price are illegal in the United States. Firms, therefore, may choose more costly means such as advertising restrictions to acquire anticompetitive gains. The costs, therefore, could be thought of as dissipation of anticompetitive gains, consistent with the work of Tullock (1967) and Posner (1975).

marginal costs of providing y value to consumers. As long as (12) holds the firms have an incentive to restrict advertising; therefore we submit,

PROPOSITION 2: *Under the demand structure (7) and (8), and with firms assuming B(m) constant, an advertising restriction will be profitable for firms as long as (12) is satisfied.*

The following example helps to illuminate the incentive to restrict advertising. Let $B(m) = a - b \cdot m$, $C(x_i) = c \cdot x_i^\beta$, and $A(a_i) = d \cdot a_i^\delta$. In our advertising function, either d or δ could play the role of θ in the preceding analysis. The parameter δ represents the elasticity of demand with respect to advertising expenditures. The parameter d provides a scaling factor for the advertising function. In either case, for a given level of advertising expenditures, demand increases as either d or δ increases.

The first step entails finding $h(y_i)$. By substituting the specific cost and advertising functions into (9), minimizing with respect to a, and substituting the solution back into (9), we have $h(y_i) = k d^{-\lambda} y_i^\lambda$ where $\lambda = \beta/(\beta\delta + \alpha)$ and

$$k = c \left[\frac{c\beta\delta}{\alpha} \right]^{-\frac{\beta\delta}{\beta\delta + \alpha}} + \left[\frac{c\beta\delta}{\alpha} \right]^{\frac{\alpha}{\beta\delta + \alpha}}.$$

Then using (10), we can solve for y_i^*. Given the demand relationship, it is not possible to solve for y_i^* explicitly, so we have given the parameters specific values and determined the change in profits by using (11). Letting $I = 50$, $b = .025$,

17

$\alpha = 1/2$, $n = 50$, $c = 1$, $\beta = 2$, $d = 1$, and $\delta = 3/8$, we find that each firm produces 13.912 units of y_i and the total profits for all firms is 3,970.

To find the effects of advertising restrictions, we first decrease the scaling factor (d) and then the advertising expenditure elasticity (δ). By reducing d from 1 to 0.9, we find that the sales (as measured by y_i) of each firm decline to 13.061 and total profits for the firms increases to 4,248. Holding d at 1 and lowering δ from 3/8ths to 1/3rd reduces sales to 11.994 and increases total profits to 5,001. Therefore, under the assumed structure and parameters, changes that make each advertising dollar spent less effective in raising demand, actually lead to higher profits.

The following figures help to elucidate how an advertising restriction may increases profits. In Figure 1, the advertising restrictions are depicted by upward shifts in the supply curves of the y output. Because the supply curves increase to a greater extent at the market level of output than closer to the origin, price increases to a greater extent than average costs, resulting in higher profits. It is important to note that profits do not increase because firms spend less on advertising. Under the assumed parameters, each restriction raises the level of advertising expenditures as measured by a_i. The restrictions, however, raise the cost of supplying the y output and result in less information being supplied to consumers, measured by a reduction in $A(a_i)$.

Figure 2 provides additional insights by showing the effects of the restrictions in Price--X output space. The marginal cost curve is simply the

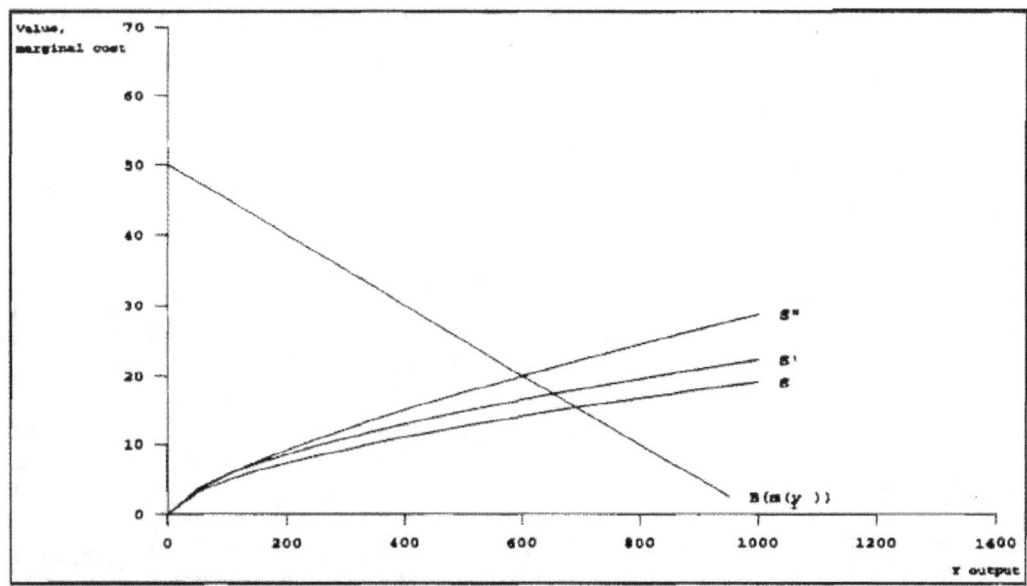

Figure 1 -- Raising marginal costs

horizontal aggregation of the individual marginal cost curves. The market demand curves are more complicated because they are a function of a_i, and cost minimization results in a different a_i for each level of output. The figure depicts demand curves with a_i's selected at their equilibrium levels given the base case and the two restrictions.

The restrictions do not affect the market marginal cost curve; rather, the restrictions only affect the demand curve. Counter-intuitively, the restrictions make demand more elastic and actually increase demand at the equilibrium level of output. The reason for this is that under the assumed value function (10), information $(A(a_i))$ obtained from advertising is a substitute for the output as

19

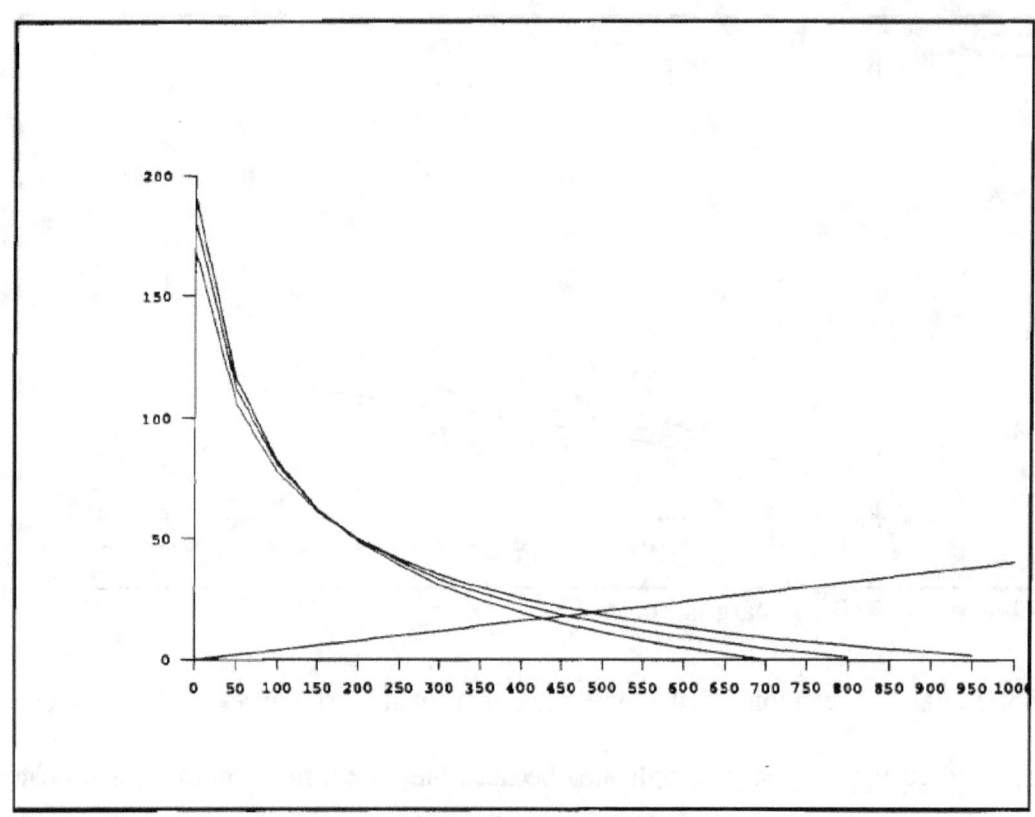

Figure 2 -- Advertisement restriction in Price-X Space

measured by x_i.[9] Therefore, at low price levels consumers compensate for

---

[9] For descriptions of how product attributes affect demand curves, see Spence (1975) and Leffler (1982). Schneider, Klein, and Murphy (1981, n. 43) conjectured that an advertising restriction may increase demand if the advertised attribute was a close substitute for the purchased good. Our analysis is consistent with their intuition. If the advertised attribute and the purchased good were complements, then the market demand would become less elastic as in the search cost models. We have worked through the analysis with $A(a_i)$ and x_i as perfect complements ($y_i = min \{A(a_i), x_i\}$). All of the qualitative results of the analysis remain with the exception that demand shifts left at the equilibrium level of output in response to lower $A(a_i)$.

reduced information by purchasing more of the product.[10] Consider advertising by doctors that reveals the set of procedures performed by each doctor. An advertising restriction which reduces the amount of information received by consumers will result in consumers making more errors in their selection of doctors. Thus, on average the expected benefit of a visit to a doctor declines. But the total number of doctor visits, measured by x_i, may increase because each visit is more likely to result in a referral to another doctor.[11] Another way to consider demands becoming more elastic with an advertising restriction is that with the restriction consumers have less information on the attributes of each product and price becomes relatively more important in the purchasing decision. Therefore, consumers are more price sensitive and demand becomes more

---

[10] Alternative information sources may develop to compensate for the reduction in information. For example, the government may attempt to directly supply health and nutritional information about food. Alternative information sources are unlikely to be perfect substitutes for information supplied through advertising. Ippolito and Mathios (1989) found significant changes in cereal consumption when ready-to-eat cereal producers began providing health information in their advertising.

[11] Notice that the output measure "procedures performed" would decrease because on average consumers expect each procedure to cost more. Part of the additional cost is the expected costs of the errors in selecting doctors.

elastic.[12] This shift is consistent with those who argue that advertising makes demand less elastic.[13]

More elastic demand from advertising restrictions is the opposite effect of that predicted by the search cost theory. Search cost theories posit that with less information in the market, consumers know fewer locations and prices of sellers and become less sensitive to differences in price. Firms respond by raising price and consumers on average purchase fewer units of the good. But in the above example the opposite occurs. With less information, market demand becomes more elastic. Price increases because demand increases at the equilibrium level of output. This, in theory, provides a possible method of distinguishing between search cost theories and the one presented here. Under search cost theories, for example, areas with advertising restrictions should sell fewer units than areas with no restrictions; while the opposite may occur under the theory presented here.[14]

---

[12] Consider the case where $A(a_i, \theta)$ is taken to be the clarity of an IO textbook. If textbooks and clarity are substitutes, then consumers would purchase multiple texts to master IO concepts. Jean Tirole could increase demand for his textbook by increasing its clarity. But if all authors of IO textbooks increase their clarity, consumers may purchase fewer texts in total because they need to consult fewer texts to understand concepts. Consumers would purchase fewer texts and receive greater value for each text.

[13] Comanor and Wilson (1974), Chapter 3.

[14] Other theories of advertising also predict fewer sales from increased costs of advertising (Friedman, 1983).

C. Nash Conjectures

We now discuss the effects of advertising restrictions when firms have Nash conjectures in y_i. That is, each firm takes account of its own actions on $B(m)$ and assumes that other firms do not react to its actions. The only change in the preceding analysis is that firms select output y_i so that marginal revenue equals marginal cost which is less than $B(m)$. Therefore, (10) becomes

$$B(\frac{1}{\alpha} \cdot \sum_{j=1}^{n} y_j^N) + B'(\frac{1}{\alpha} \cdot \sum_{j=1}^{n} y_j^N) \cdot \frac{1}{\alpha} \cdot y_i^N \equiv h_y(y_i^N, \theta),$$

where y_i^N represents the Nash level of output for each firm. Then, preceding as before, the firms would find an advertising restriction profitable as long as

$$h_{y\theta} + h_{yy} y_{i\theta}^N - B'' \frac{y_{i\theta}^N}{\alpha} y_i^N - 2 B' \frac{y_{i\theta}^N}{\alpha} < \frac{h_\theta}{y_i^N}. \tag{13}$$

And this gives,

PROPOSITION 3: *Under the demand structure (7) and (8) with Nash conjectures, an advertising restriction will be profitable for firms as long as (13) is satisfied.*

With many firms in a market we would expect the Nash outcome to be close to the prior competitive outcome, and our numerical example confirms this result. Under the base assumptions, Nash conjectures decreases firm output from 13.912 to 13.695 and profits increase to 4,341. By reducing d to 0.9, firm output falls to 12.866 and profits increase to 4,561. By reducing δ to 1/3rd, output falls to 11.834 and profits increase to 5,237.

IV. CONCLUSION

This paper has explored how advertising restrictions can behave as rent increasing costs. Section II gave the general conditions for cost increases to raise the profits of incumbent firms producing a homogenous good. Then Section III shows how advertising restrictions can act a method of raising rent increasing costs.

Several previous analysis of advertising have demonstrated that cost increases for advertising can lead to higher prices and increased profits for firms. This paper demonstrates a similar result for when advertising provides valuable information to consumers. Advertising restrictions raise the costs of firms providing value to consumers. Because the restrictions can raise the marginal costs of value to a greater extent than average costs, the restrictions can be profitable. When viewed from the supply and demand conditions for the purchased good, the restrictions can make the market demand more elastic and increase demand at the market level of output. Therefore, the observed effects of the restriction are higher prices and, surprisingly, greater sales.

REFERENCES

Benham, Lee. "The Effect of Advertising on the Price of Eyeglasses." Journal of Law and Economics 15 (October 1972): 337-52.

Bond, Ronald et al. Effects of Restrictions on Advertising and Commercial Practice in the Professions: The Case of Optometry. Washington, D.C.: Federal Trade Commission, September, 1980.

Butters, Gerard. "Equilibrium Distribution of Sales and Advertising Prices." Review of Economic Studies 44 (October 1977): 465-91.

Cady, John F. "An Estimate of the Price Effects of Restrictions on Drug Price Advertising." Economic Inquiry (1976): 493-510.

Comanor, William S. and Wilson, Thomas A. Advertising and Market Power. Cambridge: Harvard Univ. Press, 1974.

Diamond, Peter A. "A Model of Price Adjustment." Journal of Economic Theory 3 (1971): 156-68.

Friedman, James W. Oligopoly Theory. Cambridge: Cambridge Univ. Press, 1983.

Grossman, Gene M. and Shapiro, Carl. "Informative Advertising with Differentiated Products." Review of Economic Studies 51 (January 1984): 63-81.

Ippolito, Pauline and Mathios, Alan. Health Claims in Advertising and Labeling. Washington, D.C.: Federal Trade Commission, August, 1989.

Kwoka, John E., Jr. "Advertising and the Price and Quality of Optometric Services." American Economic Review 74 (March 1984): 211-6.

Langenfeld, James A. and Morris, John R. "Horizontal Restraint Cases at the Federal Trade Commission: From American Medical Association Through the Present." Presented at the 60th Annual Conference of the Southern Economics Association, New Orleans, Louisiana, November 20, 1990.

_____. "Rent Increasing Costs: The Implications for Antitrust from a Paradox of Value Theory." FTC Working Paper No. 182, November 1990.

Leffler, Keith B. "Ambiguous Changes in Product Quality." American Economic Review 72 (December 1982): 956-67.

Maloney, Michael T., McCormick, Robert E., and Tollison, Robert D. "Achieving Cartel Profits Through Unionization." Southern Economic Journal 46 (October 1979): 628-34.

Maurizi, Alex and Kelly, Thom. Prices and Consumer Information: The Benefits from Posting Retail Gasoline Price. Washington, D.C.: American Enterprise Institute. 1978.

Nelson, Richard R. "Increased Rents from Increased Costs: A Paradox of Value Theory." Journal of Political Economy 65(5) (October 1957): 387-93.

Posner, Richard A. "The Social Costs of Monopoly and Regulation." Journal of Political Economy 83 (August 1975): 807-27.

Salop, Steven C., Scheffman, David T. and Schwartz, Warren. "A Bidding Analysis of Special Interest Regulation: Raising Rivals' Costs in a Rent Seeking Society." in The Political Economy of Regulation: Private Interests in the Regulatory Process. Washington, D.C.: Federal Trade Commission. 1984.

Scheffman, David T. "The Application of Raising Rivals' Costs Theory to Antitrust." Antitrust Bulletin 36 (Summer 1991): forthcoming.

Schneider, Lynne; Klein, Benjamin; and Murphy, Kevin M. "Government Regulation of Cigarette Health Information." Journal of Law and Economics 24 (December 1981): 575-612.

Schroeter, John R., Smith, L., Scott, L., and Cox, Steven R., "Advertising and Competition in Routine Legal Service Markets: An Empirical Investigation," Journal of Industrial Economics, 36 (September 1987): 49-60.

Spence, A. Michael. "Monopoly, Quality, and Regulation." Bell Journal of Economics 6 (Autumn 1975): 417-29.

_____. "Notes on Advertising, Economies of Scale, and Entry Barriers." Quarterly Journal of Economics 95 (November 1980): 493-507.

Stahl, Dale O., II. "Oligopolistic Pricing with Sequential Consumer Search." American Economic Review 79 (September 1989): 700-712.

Stigler, George J. and Becker, Gary S. *"De Gustibus Non Est Disputandum."* American Economic Review 67 (March 1977): 76-90.

Tirole, Jean. The Theory of Industrial Organization. Cambridge, Mass.: MIT Press. 1988.

Tullock, Gordon. "The Welfare Costs of Tariffs, Monopolies, and Theft." Western Economic Journal 5 (1967): 224-32.

Varian, Hal R. "A Model of Sales." American Economic Review 70 (September 1980): 651-59.

www.ingramcontent.com/pod-product-compliance
Lightning Source LLC
Chambersburg PA
CBHW081318180526

45170CB00007B/2761